MW01177912

I care.
May this pure and simple message of
hope lift you up today.

To: _____

From: _____

Date: _____

Compliments of the
"Television Ministry"
The Peoples Church, Toronto
Watch Dr. John Hull weekly
Check your local TV Listings

Tomorrow's DREAM Today's COURAGE

MAX LUCADO

WORD PUBLISHING

Dallas · London · Vancouver · Melbourne

Tomorrow's Dream, Today's Courage

Published by Word Publishing

© 1995 by Max Lucado

All rights reserved. No part of this publication may be reproduced,
stored in a retrieval system, or transmitted in any form or by any
means–electronic, mechanical, photocopy, recording, or
any other–except for brief quotations in printed reviews,
without the prior permission of the publisher.

"Pilgrim Ponderings" and " Our Storm was His Path" from
In the Eye of the Storm © 1991 by Max Lucado; "The Bandit of Joy"
from *The Applause of Heaven* © 1990 by Max Lucado.
ISBN 08499-5212-3

Printed in the United States of America

For information about "UpWords" radio
ministry featuring Max Lucado, write:

P. O. Box 5860
San Antonio, TX 78201

Tomorrow's Dream, Today's Courage

· · · · · · ·

*C*HILDHOOD NIGHTS: *shadows on the wall, boogey-men in the closet, and scary things going bump.*

Conquering the boogey-man was pretty easy back then—all it took was a plaintive "Mommee" or "Dadee" and help was on the way. A parental peek under the bed, a reassuring kiss, a nightlight, and . . . Whew! "It" was gone . . . at least until the next night.

Now that you're grown up, you've defeated all your fears . . . right? Yeah, right. The "its" of nighttime have become full-fledged attack squadrons of anxiety. And shadows on the wall don't always disappear with the dawn.

When you holler for help, sometimes all you hear is your own cry echoing down a lonely corridor. So what to you do? When your dreams are darkened by broken promises, unfulfilled expectations, or a hardened heart . . . when giving up seems like the only option left . . . what do you do?

There is a source of renewed courage. There is a wellspring of faith just waiting to be tapped.

So, drink deeply . . . it's not too late for tomorrow's dream to become today's courage.

Chapter One

Pilgrim Ponderings

AFTER SIX days Jesus took with him Peter, James and John the brother of James, and led them up a high mountain by themselves. There he was transfigured before them. His face shone like the sun, and his clothes became as white as the light. Just then there appeared before them Moses and Elijah, talking with Jesus.

Peter said to Jesus, "Lord, it is good for us to be here. If you wish, I will put up three shelters—one for you, one for Moses, and one for Elijah." While he was still speaking, a bright cloud enveloped them, and a voice from the cloud said, "This is my Son, whom I love; with him I am well pleased. Listen to him!"[1]

ॐ

The young woman, eight months heavy with child, waddles into her mother's house. Flops onto the sofa. Kicks off her tennis shoes. Props her puffy feet on the coffee table. And groans, "I don't think I can make it."

Wise from the years, the mother picks up a photo album and sits down beside her daughter. She opens the album to photos of her children in diapers and ankle-high walking shoes. Slowly the two turn the memory-filled pages. They smile at the kids blowing out candles and sitting in front of Christmas trees.

As the mother sees yesterday, the daughter sees tomorrow.

And, for just a moment, the daughter is changed. The *here and now* becomes the *there and then.* Her child is born. She sees the first stumbling step taken. She hears the first word, discernible only to Mommy. She places the shiny, black, patent-leather shoes on the stockinged feet and Karo-syrups a ribbon on the nearly bald but ever-so-precious head.

A transformation occurs. The pain in her back is now overshadowed by the joy approaching. The hand that had rubbed the neck now rests on her stomach. For the first time that day, she smiles.

❧

A snowstorm in Chicago. Stranded at O'Hare. No place to sit in the lobby, so he walks to the coffee shop. No place to sit in the coffee shop, so he buys a cup to go, wanders back to the lobby, sits on his briefcase, and drapes his overcoat over his lap.

He looks at his watch. *Should I go to a hotel for the night?* he wonders. *It's nearly midnight! I should be halfway home by now. Who knows when I'll be able to leave?*

He sighs, leans back against a wall, and waits. He unbuttons his collar. Loosens his tie. Rubs his whiskered neck. His thoughts drift back over the week. Many calls made. Few orders placed. Blame it on the economy. Blame it on the system. Blame it on God. But blame doesn't put money in the bank.

There's an executive lobby across the hall with empty couches, snacks, and a television. In better times, he could afford the membership; now that money goes toward college tuition and braces for the kids.

A flight is announced. He pulls his boarding pass out of his overcoat breast pocket. The flight isn't his. He sticks the pass back into the coat that stretches across his lap. A leather calendar tumbles. He picks it up and, for no real reason, looks inside.

There, amidst taxi receipts and credit cards, is a laminated photo of a family—his family. Teenage daughter with eyes like her mom's and the metallic smile. College-bound son wearing a necktie and blue jeans, mid-step between adolescence and adulthood. And his wife. My, has it been twenty-five years? Take away a few wrinkles and pounds, and he can see her in the white gown again.

For just a moment, he is home. The television is off. The kids are in bed. The dog is outside. The doors are locked. The fire is golden. His wife is asleep on the couch. For just a moment, the world of O'Hare, hotels, and sales calls are a world away. He is where it's all worthwhile. He is home.

Someone taps him on the shoulder, and he hears a kind voice. "Is that your flight?" He looks up into the half-empty lobby . . . sees the line forming at the gate . . . and smiles.

"Yeah," the salesman says, standing. "It's my flight home."

Four people snake their way up the mountain. The trip has been long; the hour is late. A level place on the hillside is reached, and they sit down. They're tired. Their muscles hurt. The grayness of twilight settles over them like a soft cloth.

The quartet of pilgrims longs to sleep, but only three do.

The fourth sits in the shadows. Legs crossed. Face skyward. The stars wink at their Maker. Winds waft over the shoulders of their Designer, cooling his neck. He slips off his sandals and rubs his sore feet and reflects on the wildness of it all.

A God with sore legs? Holiness with hunger? Divinity with thirst? A World Maker made weary by his world?

His thoughts drift homeward. *Nazareth. How good it would be to be home again.*

The memories surface so easily. Sawdust-covered workbench. Friends stopping to talk. Dinner-table laughter. Wrestling with his brothers. The synagogue. The house. The home.

What I'd give to go home.

But Nazareth would never be home again. They tried to kill him the last time he was there. Neighbors, friends, teachers, schoolmates . . . they squeezed the stones intended for his body. Even his brothers and sisters considered him insane. They wanted to hide him, to put him away. They were ashamed to be known as his family.

No, Nazareth can never be home again.

What about Galilee? He could go back to Galilee. There the crowds listened. There the people followed. But he shook his head. *As long as I made them bread . . . As long as I said what they wanted to hear . . .* He remembered the crowds as they turned away. He heard their jeering. He felt their rejection.

No, I can never go back to Galilee.

He thinks of Jerusalem. She offers no comfort. He knows what she will do to him. A foreboding pain stabs his wrists. He winces at the slicing of his brow. He sees the world around him growing darker, darker . . . *My God!* a premonition inside him cries.

He shakes his head and breathes a staggered breath. His thoughts return to the present.

He plucks a shoot of grass, puts it into his mouth, and sits in the shadow of his fear.

He looks at his followers, as asleep as they are naive. They have no idea. They just can't understand. He speaks of suffering; they think of conquering. He speaks of sacrifice; they think of celebration. He's an artist painting for the color-blind. He's a singer singing for the deaf. They nod their heads and clap their hands. They think they see. They think they hear. But they don't.

They can't see. No one sees.

Part of him knew it would be like this. And part of him never knew it would be so bad.

Part of him wonders, *Would it be so bad to give up?* After all, there might be a better era. There will be other generations . . . other people.

He has given his best, and what does he have? A ragged band of good-hearted but hardheaded followers who are destined to fall face-flat over promises they can't keep. He puts his face into his cupped hands and closes his eyes and prays. It's all he knows to do.

❧

Sounds familiar, doesn't it, seeker? Was it so long ago that you were on a quest for truth—Galahad in search of the grail? But the forest of questions was deep. The thicket of perplexities thick. It was easier to say nothing than to ask why. So you stopped.

Sounds familiar, doesn't it, dreamer? You wanted so badly to change the world. Sure the mountain was high, but you were brave. Then the winds came. Sharp rocks of reality cut your feet, breaking your stride . . . breaking your heart. And you found that the role of the cynic was less costly than the role of the dreamer. So you sat down.

You need to know something: Jesus sat down, too.

Oh, sure, there were moments when he stood tall. There were hours of splendor. There were dynamic days during which the lepers leapt and the dead came alive and the people worshiped. Those days came.

But his plateaus of popularity were gorged by canyons of isolation.

And on this day, the crevasse is deep. Steep walls mock an easy escape. Rocky abutments imprison his vision. His strength has reached its solstice.

He sits down and puts a tear-streaked face into cupped palms and prays. It's all he can do.

And when his Father sees him, it's all his Father can take.

From another dimension, a light comes. It enters the solitary figure and glows.

"As he was praying," Luke writes, "the appearance of his face changed, and his clothes became as bright as a flash of lightning."[2]

Jesus implodes with glory. For just a moment, he is transfigured; a roaring radiance pours from him. He becomes as he was before he came. For one brief, shining moment, the burden of his humanity is lifted. "Decarnation" occurs. He is elevated above earth's horizon and escorted into the eternal. He is home again. Familiar sounds surround him. Those who understand welcome him. And the One who sent him . . . holds him.

Dusty trails and hard hearts are, literally, a world away.

The One who felt weary is reminded: the weariness will soon pass.

Moses and Elijah, aflame with eternal robes, stand beside their King. When Jesus was preparing himself in the desert for the work of life, angels came to encourage him. Now, on the mountain, preparing himself for the work of death, Moses and Elijah draw near: Moses, the Lawgiver whose grave no man knew; Elijah, the prophet who sidestepped death in a fiery chariot.

The One who saw death is reminded: the grave is impotent.

And then, the voice thunders. God inhabits a cloud. It becomes a bonfire, puffy with brilliance. It consumes the shadows. It trans-forms the nightened mountain into a shining monument. And from the belly of the cloud, the Father speaks:

"This is my Son, whom I love; with him I am well pleased. Listen to him!"[3]

The One who had despaired is affirmed. "What people think doesn't matter," God shouts. "What I think does. And I'm proud."

By now Jesus is standing. By now the apostles are awake.

For Peter, James, and John, the scene is bizarre: dazzling white clouds, a voice from the sky, living images from the past. But for Jesus, it is a view of home. A view into yesterday. A glimpse into tomorrow.

He is the mother—pregnant with new life, dreading the pains of childbirth.

He is the father—on a long journey in a cold place.

He is—as they were, as we are—given a glimpse of home.

And tomorrow's dream becomes today's courage.

Chapter Two

. . . .

Our Storm Was His Path

SUPPOSE ONE of Jesus' disciples kept a journal. And suppose that disciple made an entry in the journal on the morning after the storm. And suppose we discovered that journal. Here is how it would read . . . I suppose.

෨

Only minutes before, chaos had erupted.

Oh, how the storm roared. Stars were hidden by a black ceiling. Clouds billowed like smoke. Bolts of lightning were the conductor's baton that cued the kettledrums of thunder to rumble.

And rumble they did. The clouds seemed to rise as a bear on hind legs and growl. The booms shook everything: the heavens, the earth, and—most of all—the sea. It was as if the Sea of Galilee were a bowl in the hands of a dancing giant. From the bowels of the lake the waves came, turning the glassy surface into a mountain range of snow-topped waves. Five, ten, even fifteen feet into the air they mounted, rising and falling like swallows chasing mosquitoes.

In the midst of the sea, our boat bounced. The waves slapped it as easily as children would a ball. Our straining at the oars scarcely budged it. We were at the storm's mercy. The waves lifted us up so high that we felt like we were in midair. Then down into the valley we plunged.

We were a twig in a whirlpool . . . a leaf in the wind. We were helpless.

That's when the light appeared. At first I thought it was a reflection of the moon, a gleam on the surface of the water. But the night held no moon. I looked again. The light was moving toward us, not over the waves but through them. I wasn't the only one who saw it.

"A ghost," someone screamed. Fear of the sea was eclipsed by a new terror. Thoughts raced as the specter drew near. *Was it a figment of our imagination? Was it a vision? Who? How? What was this mystical light that appeared so . . . ?*

A flash of lightning illuminated the sky. For a second I could see its face . . . his face. A second was all I needed.

It was the Master!

He spoke:

"Take courage! It is I. Don't be afraid."[1]

Nothing had changed. The storm still raged. The wind still shrieked. The boat still pitched. The thunder still boomed. The rain still slapped. But in the midst of the tumult, I could hear his voice. Although he was still far away, it was like he was by my side. The night was ferocious, yet he spoke as though the sea were placid and the sky silent.

And, somehow, courage came.

"Lord, if it's you, . . . tell me to come to you on the water."[2]

The voice was Peter's. He wasn't being cocky. He wasn't demanding proof. He was scared. Like me, he knew what this storm could do. He knew that the boat would soon go down. He knew that Jesus was standing up. And he knew where he wanted to be . . . where we all wanted to be.

"Come on," Jesus invited.

So Peter climbed over the side and stepped onto the sea. Before him opened a trail through a forest of waves. He stepped quickly. Water splashed. But he kept going. This path to Jesus was a ribbon of calm. It was peaceful. Serene.

Jesus radiated light at the end of the trail. Smiling.

Peter stepped toward the light like it was his only hope. He was halfway there when we all heard the thunder. It boomed, and he stopped. I saw his head turn. He looked up at the sky. He looked up at the clouds. He felt the wind. And down he went.

Boy did he yell!

A hand came through the water sheets and grabbed Peter. Lightning flashed again, and I could see the face of Jesus. I noticed that his smile was gone. Hurt covered his face. It was like he couldn't believe that we couldn't believe. Danger to us was just a detour to him. I wanted to ask him, "Aren't you afraid, Jesus? Aren't you afraid?"

But I said nothing. Before I knew it, he was in the boat with us.

The sea stilled as silk.

The winds hushed.

A canyon opened in the clouds; soft moonlight fell over the water.

It happened instantaneously. It didn't take the rest of the night. It didn't take an hour. It didn't take a minute. It happened in a blink.

From chaos to calm. From panic to peace. The sky was so suddenly silent that I could hear my heart pounding. I thought I was dreaming. Then I saw the wide eyes of the others and felt my clothing soaked against my skin. This was no dream. I looked at the water. I looked at Peter. I looked at the others. And then I looked at him.

And I did the only thing I could have done. With the stars as my candles and the stilled boat as my altar, I fell at his feet and worshiped.

There are times in a person's life when, even in the midst of them, you know you'll never be the same. Moments that forever serve as journey posts. This was one.

I had never seen Jesus as I saw him then. I had seen him as powerful. I had seen him as wise. I had witnessed his authority and marveled at his abilities. But what I witnessed last night, I know I'll never forget.

I saw God. The God who can't sit still when the storm is too strong. The God who lets me get frightened enough to need him and then comes close enough for me to see him. The God who uses my storms as his path to come to me.

I saw God. It took a storm for me to see him. But I saw him. And I'll never be the same.

Chapter Three

· · · · · · ·

The Bandit of Joy

H E WAS A professional thief. His name stirred fear as the desert wind stirs tumbleweeds. He terrorized the Wells Fargo stage line for thirteen years, roaring like a tornado in and out of the Sierra Nevadas, spooking the most rugged frontiersmen. In journals from San Francisco to New York, his name became synonymous with the danger of the frontier.

During his reign of terror between 1875 and 1883, he is credited with stealing the bags and the breath away from twenty-nine different stagecoach crews. And he did it all without firing a shot.

His weapon was his reputation. His ammunition was intimidation.

A hood hid his face. No victim ever saw him. No artist ever sketched his features. No sheriff could ever track his trail. He never fired a shot or took a hostage.

He didn't have to. His presence was enough to paralyze.

Black Bart. A hooded bandit armed with a deadly weapon.

He reminds me of another thief—one who's still around. You know him. Oh you've never seen his face, either. You couldn't describe his voice or sketch his profile. But when he's near, you know it in a heartbeat.

If you've ever been in the hospital, you've felt the leathery brush of his hand against yours.

If you've ever sensed someone was following you, you've felt his cold breath down your neck.

If you've awakened late at night in a strange room, it was his husky whisper that stole your slumber.

You know him.

It was this thief who left your palms sweaty as you went for the job interview.

It was this con man who convinced you to swap your integrity for popularity.

And it was this scoundrel who whispered in your ear as you left the cemetery, "You may be next."

He's the Black Bart of the soul. He doesn't want your money. He doesn't want your diamonds. He won't go after your car. He wants something far more precious. He wants your peace of mind—your joy.

His name?

Fear.

His task is to take your courage and leave you timid and trembling. His *modus operandi is* to manipulate you with the mysterious, to taunt you with the unknown. Fear of death, fear of failure, fear of God, fear of tomorrow—his arsenal is vast. His goal? To create cowardly, joyless souls.

He doesn't want you to make the journey to the mountain. He figures if he can rattle you enough, you will take your eyes off the peaks and settle for a dull existence in the flatlands.

❧

A legend from India tells about a mouse who was terrified of cats until a magician agreed to transform him into a cat. That resolved his fear . . . until he met a dog, so the magician changed him into a dog. The mouse-turned-cat-turned-dog was content until he met a tiger—so, once again, the magician changed him into what he feared. But when the tiger came complaining that he had met a hunter, the magician refused to help. "I will make you into a mouse again, for though you have the body of a tiger, you still have the heart of a mouse."

Sound familiar? How many people do you know who have built a formidable exterior, only to tremble inside with fear? We tackle our anxieties by taking on the appearance of a tiger. We face our fears with force. Military power, security systems, defense strategy—all reflect a conviction that muscle creates security.

Or if we don't use force, we try other methods. We stockpile wealth. We seek security in things. We cultivate fame and seek status.

But do these approaches work? Can power, possessions, or popularity really deliver us from our fears?

If power could, then Joseph Stalin should have been fearless. Instead, this infamous Russian premier was afraid to go bed. He had seven different bedrooms. Each could be locked as tightly as a safe. In order to foil any would-be assassins, he slept in a different one each night. Five chauffeur-driven limousines transported him wherever he went, each with curtains closed so no one would know which contained Stalin. So deep-seated were his apprehensions that he employed a servant whose sole task was to monitor and protect his tea bags.[1]

If possessions conquered fear, the late billionaire Howard Hughes would have been fearless. But you probably know his story. His distrust of people and his paranoia of germs led this billionaire to Mexico, where he died a lonely death as a cadaverous hermit with a belly-length beard and corkscrew fingernails.[2]

What about popularity? Beatle John Lennon's fame as a singer, songwriter, and pop icon made him a household word, but his fears brought him misery. His biographers describe him as a frightened man, unwilling to sleep with the lights off and afraid to touch anything because of its filth.[3]

Though Stalin, Hughes, and Lennon are extreme cases, they are indicative ones. "Though you have the body of a tiger, you still have the heart of a mouse."

Parallel their stories with the life of a little-known but gutsy young man named Paul Keating. On a cold night in February 1980, twenty-seven-year-old Keating was walking home in Manhattan's Greenwich Village when he saw two armed muggers robbing a college student. Keating, a gentle, much-admired photographer for *Time* magazine, had every reason to avoid trouble. He didn't know the student. No one knew he saw the crime. He was outnumbered. He had nothing to gain and much to lose by taking the risk, and yet he jumped on the muggers. The victim escaped and ran to a nearby deli to call for help. Moments later, two shots cracked the night, and the muggers fled. Paul Keating was found dead on the pavement.

The city of New York posthumously awarded him a medal of heroism. I think you'll agree with the commentary offered by Mayor Edward Koch at the ceremony: "Nobody was watching Paul Keating on the street that night. Nobody made him step forward in the time of crisis. He did it because of who he was."[4]

Well put.

Courage is an outgrowth of who we are. Exterior supports may temporarily sustain, but only inward character creates courage.

And it is those inward convictions that Jesus is building in the Beatitudes. Remember, Matthew 5 is not a list of proverbs or a compilation of independent sayings, but rather a step-by-step description of how God rebuilds the believer's heart.

The first step is to ask for help—to become "poor in spirit" and admit our need for a Savior.

The next step is sorrow: "Blessed are those who mourn . . ." Those who mourn are those who know they are wrong and say they are sorry. No excuses. No justification. Just tears.

The first two steps are admittance of inadequacy and repentance for pride. The next step is the one of renewal: "Blessed are the meek . . ." Realization of weakness leads to the source of strength—God. And renewal comes when we become meek—when we give our lives to God to be his tool.

The first two beatitudes pass us through the fire of purification; the third places us in the hands of the Master.

The result of this process? Courage: ". . . they shall inherit the earth." No longer shall the earth and its fears dominate us, for we follow the one who dominates the earth.

❧

Could you use some courage? Are you backing down more than you are standing up? If so, let the Master lead you up the mountain again. Let him remind you why you should "fear not." Listen to the time Jesus scattered the butterflies out of the stomachs of his nervous disciples and see if his words help you.[5]

We need to remember that the disciples were common men given a compelling task. Before they were the stained-glassed saints in the windows of cathedrals, they were somebody's next-door-neighbors trying to make a living and raise a family. They weren't cut from theological cloth or raised on supernatural milk. But they were an ounce more devoted than they were afraid and, as a result, did some extraordinary things.

They would have done nothing, however, had they not learned to face their fears. Jesus knew that. That is why he spoke his words of courage.

The disciples are being sent out on their own. For a limited time they will go into the cities and do what Jesus has done—but without Jesus. Jesus assembles them to give them the final instructions. Perhaps the disciples look nervous, for they have reason to be nervous. What Jesus tells them would raise the pulse rate of the stoutest heart.

First Jesus tells them not to take any extra money or extra clothing on their journey.

"No money?"

Then he assures them that they are being sent out "like sheep among wolves."

"Uh, what do you mean, Jesus?"

His answer is not reassuring. He tells them they will be taken before the authorities, (uh-oh), flogged, (ouch), and arrested (groan).

And it gets worse before it gets better.

Jesus goes on to describe the impact their mission will have on people: "Brother will betray brother to death, and a father his child; children will rebel against their parents and have them put to death. All men will hate you because of me, but he who stands firm to the end will be saved."[6]

Some eyes duck. Some eyes widen. Someone swallows. Feet shift. A brow is wiped. And though no one says it, you know someone is thinking, "Is it too late to get out of this?"

That's the setting for Jesus' paragraph on courage. Three times in five verses[7] he says, "Do not be afraid. Read the words and see his call and cause for courage. See the reason you should sleep well tonight:

"So do not be afraid of them. There is nothing concealed that will not be disclosed, or hidden that will not be made known."[8]

On the surface, those words would seem like a reason for panic rather than a source of peace. Who of us would like to have our secret thoughts made public? Who would want our private sins published? Who would get excited over the idea that every wrong deed we've ever done will be announced to everyone?

You're right, no one would. But we're told over and over that such a thing *will* happen:

> Nothing in all creation is hidden from God's sight. Everything is uncovered and laid bare before the eyes of him to whom we must give account.

> He reveals deep and hidden things; he knows what lies in darkness, and light dwells with him.

> But I tell you that men will have to give account on the day of judgment for every careless word they have spoken.

> You have set our iniquities before you, our secret sins in the light of your presence.

> He will bring to light what is hidden in darkness and will expose the motives of men's hearts.[9]

To think of the disclosure of my hidden heart conjures up emotions of shame, humiliation, and embarrassment in me. There are things I've done that I want no one to know. There are thoughts I've thought I would never want to be revealed. So why does Jesus point to the day of revelation as a reason for *courage?* How can I take strength in what should be a moment of anguish?

The answer is found in Romans 2:16. Let out a sigh of relief as you underline the last three words of the verse: "This will take place on the day when God will judge men's secrets *through Jesus Christ."*

Did you see it? Jesus is the screen through which God looks when he judges our sins. Now read another chorus of verses and focus on their promise:

> Therefore, there is now no condemnation for those who are in Christ Jesus.
>
> [God] justifies those who have faith in Jesus.
>
> Through him everyone who believes is justified from everything.
>
> For I will forgive their wickedness and will remember their sins no more.
>
> For you died, and your life is now hidden with Christ in God.[10]

If you are in Christ, these promises are not only a source of joy. They are also the foundations of true courage. You are guaranteed that your sins will be filtered through, hidden in, and screened out by the sacrifice of Jesus. When God looks at you, he doesn't see you; he sees the One who surrounds you. That means that failure is not a concern for you. Your victory is secure. How could you not be courageous?

Picture it this way. Imagine that you are an ice skater in competition. You are in first place with one more round to go. If you perform well, the trophy is yours. You are nervous, anxious, and frightened.

Then, only minutes before your performance, your trainer rushes to you with the thrilling news: "You've already won! The judges tabulated the scores, and the person in second place can't catch you. You are too far ahead."

Upon hearing that news, how will you feel? Exhilarated!

And how will you skate? Timidly? Cautiously? Of course not. How about courageously and confidently? You bet you will. You will do your best because the prize is yours. You will skate like a champion because that is what you are! You will hear the applause of victory.

Hence, these words from Hebrews: "Therefore, brothers, since we have *confidence* to enter the Most Holy Place by the blood of Jesus . . . let us draw near to God with a sincere heart in *full assurance* of faith."[11]

The point is clear: the truth will triumph. The Father of truth will win, and the followers of truth will be saved.

As a result, Jesus says, don't be afraid:

What I tell you in the dark, speak in the daylight; what is whispered in your ear, proclaim from the roofs. Do not be afraid of those who kill the body but cannot kill the soul. Rather, be afraid of the One who can destroy both soul and body in hell. [12]

Earthly fears are no fears at all. All the mystery is revealed. The final destination is guaranteed. Answer the big question of eternity, and the little questions of life fall into perspective.

And by the way, remember Black Bart? As it turns out, he wasn't anything to be afraid of, either. When the hood came off, there was nothing to fear. When the authorities finally tracked down the thief, they didn't find a bloodthirsty bandit from Death Valley; they found a mild-mannered druggist from Decatur, Illinois. The man the papers pictured storming through the mountains on horseback was, in reality, so afraid of horses he rode to and from his robberies in a buggy. He was Charles E. Boles—the bandit who never once fired a shot, because he never once loaded his gun.[13]

Any false hoods in your world?

Study Guide
· · · · · · ·

CHAPTER ONE
PILGRIM PONDERINGS

1. Why do you think God the Father spoke to Jesus on the mountain? (See Matthew 17:1–5.)

2. What kinds of experiences make you unbearably weary, leaving you sitting on the mountainside with your face in your hands? What does it take to encourage you during those times?

3. Describe a time when God transformed your desolation and met your need in a specific way.

CHAPTER TWO
OUR STORM WAS HIS PATH

1. Has God ever used a storm "as his path to come to you"? What were the circumstances? What was the result in your life? In the lives of others around you?

2. What is your usual response when a storm lifts you up and then plunges you into a valley? Do you find it easier to sit in a tossing boat than to step out onto the water and walk toward Jesus? Why or why not?

3. When you have been desperately afraid in your life, and have seen an image coming toward you, have you ever cried out, "Lord, is it you?" If so, what was the answer? Was

it as comforting as Jesus' response in
Matthew 14:27?

4. Have you ever stepped out in faith like
   Peter did? (See Matthew 14:28–29.) Why
   did you do it? What was the result?

5. Write down a time in your life when God
   responded to your need in a special way and
   you knew you'd never be the same again.
   What did you discover about God in that
   situation that you had never seen before?

6. Most of us tend to look down on Peter's ill-
   fated walk on the water because he sank at
   the end. But at least he got out of the boat!
   In what ways can you take steps of faith and
   get out of the boat this week?

CHAPTER THREE
THE BANDIT OF JOY

1. What are the three ways we seek to handle
   our fears? To which of these three are you
   more likely to turn? (Don't be misled by the
   'big guy' examples; these defense mecha-
   nisms take many forms—major and
   minor!) Give an example of a time when
   you have taken refuge in one of these
   defenses.

2. What reason did Jesus give the disciples for
   not being afraid? Why can this be taken as a
   source of courage?

3. What would you do tomorrow if you were
   guaranteed you couldn't fail and that
   nothing could hurt you? Write down and/or
   share one example.

Notes

. . . .

Chapter 1—Pilgrim Ponderings

1. Matthew 17:1–5.

2. Luke 9:29.

3. Matthew 17:5.

Chapter 2—Our Storm Was His Path

1. Matthew 14:27.

2. Matthew 14:28.

Chapter 3—The Bandit of Joy

1. Ian Grey, *Stalin* (Garden City, NY: Doubleday, 1979), 457, and Alex De Jonge, *Stalin and the Shaping of the Soviet Union* (New York: William Morrow, 1986), 450.

2. "The Secret Life of Howard Hughes," *Time,* 13 December 1976, 22-41.

3. "John Lennon: In the Hard Day's Light," *People Weekly,* 15 August 1989, 68-69.

4. "In Praise of Courage," *Quest,* November 1980, 23.

5. See Matthew 10:1–28.

6. See Matthew 10:21–22.

7. See Matthew 10:26–31.

8. See Matthew 10:26.

9. Hebrews 4:13, Daniel 2:22, Matthew 12:36, Psalm 90:8, 1 Corinthians 4:5.

10. Romans 8:1, 3:26, Acts 13:39, Hebrews 8:12, Colossians 3:3.

11. Hebrews 10:19, 22, emphasis mine.

12. Matthew 10:27–28.

13. Paul Harvey, *Paul Harvey's The Rest of the Story* (New York, NY: Bantam, 1977), 117.